Eric Liddell

Running for God

Sue Shaw

OM Publishing
CARLISLE, UK.

ISBN 1-85078-105-2
Copyright © 1993 OM Publishing.
Design copyright © 1993 Three's
Company.
First published in Great Britain 1994.

All rights reserved. No part of this
publication may be reproduced or
transmitted in any form or by any
means, electronic or mechanical,
including photocopying, recording, or any
information storage or retrieval system,
without either prior permission in
writing from the publisher or a licence
permitting restricted copying. In the
United Kingdom such licences are issued
by the Copyright Licensing Agency, 90
Tottenham Court Road, London W1P
9HE. The right of Sue Shaw to be
identified as the author of this work has
been asserted by her in accordance with
the Copyright, Designs and Patents Act
1988.

**British Library Cataloguing in Publication
Data**

Shaw, Sue
    Eric Liddell : Running for God
    I. Title   II. Rees, Gary
    266.0092

    ISBN 1–85078–105–2

OM Publishing is an imprint of STL Ltd,
PO Box 300, Carlisle,
Cumbria CA3 0QS, UK

Designed and created by
Three's Company,
12 Flitcroft Street,
London WC2H 8DJ

Author: Sue Shaw
Illustrations by Gary Rees

Worldwide co-edition organised and
produced by
Angus Hudson Ltd,
Concorde House,
Grenville Place,
London NW7 3SA

Printed in Singapore.

'Gold medal for running 400 metres in a world record time of 47.6 seconds. Eric Liddell for Great Britain!' The crowd roared its approval. Eric stood on the centre platform as the shining gold medallion was hung round his neck.

With tears in his eyes he remembered when, as a child, he had been so ill that someone said, 'That boy will never be able to run!' Yet here he was, winner of the 1924 Olympic gold medal for the 400 metres.

Fifty years later his amazing achievement inspired the British film-maker, David Puttnam, to choose Eric as the hero of his Oscar-winning film 'Chariots of Fire'. How many children start out weak and frail and end up as Olympic gold medallists? And what was so special about Eric that a famous producer should make a film about him?

Born in 1902, Eric spent the first few years of his life in China, where his parents were working as missionaries. With his older brother Robbie and baby sister Jenny, he played with the Chinese children, learned their games and their language.

Even as a small boy he knew he was the weakest in the family. One cold winter's day, when out walking, Eric and his family were caught in a violent sand and dust storm. The dust stung their skin and the sand whipped into their eyes and almost swept them off their feet.

'We'll have to turn back!' called his father.

'It's too far. You'll have to leave me,' cried Eric, knowing that he was slowing them down.

Grabbing his hand tightly his father said, 'Hang on laddie, we'll not leave ye!' and together they struggled safely home.

When Eric was five, the family left China and returned to Scotland to spend time with their friends and relatives. Eric was amazed by the green highlands and towering trees, so different from the flat, dry, yellow Chinese plain.

'I don't think much of lessons . . .'
After a year it was time for the boys to start boarding school in London and for their parents to return to China. With his pale skin, fair hair and blue eyes, Eric looked so frail that, when he first arrived at the school, one of the teachers thought he looked rather 'weedy'.

However, the headmaster believed in lots of fresh air and plenty of exercise. Playing rugby four times a week during the winter, and cricket in the summer, Eric soon changed from a thin, shy boy into a healthy, lively and confident one.

By the time Eric was sixteen, he was captain of the rugby and cricket teams. Between them he and Robbie won nearly all the athletics races. In the 100-yard sprint, Eric set a new school record of 10.2 seconds, which has never been beaten! Secretly he admitted to his sister, 'I don't think much of lessons but I can run.'

None of this success made him big-headed, because he believed in working hard and he wanted to please God. His favourite activity was Bible class, although he was too shy to join in the discussions and preferred to think over what he had heard when he was alone.

Robbie wanted to be a doctor; but Eric's ambition was to be a missionary, like his father. Both boys were excited about working abroad, so they read lots of missionary magazines, especially any that contained news about China.

Too busy

Eric left school when he was eighteen and went to Edinburgh University to begin studying for a science degree. He had only been a student a few months when he was asked to run in the university athletics meeting. 'I'm too busy,' he replied. 'I've loads of work to do, and I've no time for that sort of thing.' It took quite a while to persuade him, but eventually he agreed to take part.

Eric was running against Innes Stewart, a man who was expected to become Scottish champion. Each race was run in several parts, called heats. The runners took their places and crouched, ready for the start of the heat for the 100 yards. The gun cracked. Innes sprang into the lead, but Eric kept right on his heels. Innes won the heat by just a couple of inches. However, in the final it was Eric's turn to win by two inches.

Eric was to race Innes in the 200 yards too. This time he was in the lead until, in the final straight, Innes put on a sudden spurt to win. Eric had no idea that this would be the only time that he ever came second in a race final at a Scottish meeting.

Eric's success earned him a place in other races all over Scotland. Soon he was breaking records and bringing home trophies and prizes. The house became jam-packed full with his collection of watches, clocks, plates, luggage, bowls, fountain pens and cutlery.

Whenever he raced, crowds turned up to watch. His running style was unlike anything seen before. He ran with his arms waving wildly, and his head so far back he seemed to be looking at the sky. His knees came up as if he was trying to hit his chin, and he lifted his feet too high off the ground. But still he won, and he was soon the best-known athlete in Scotland.

Have a good race!

About this time, Eric was asked to speak in public about his
faith in God, something he had never done before. In a quiet,
firm voice Eric addressed the large crowd. 'It's a great thing to
know for sure that God loves me,' he said. 'I want you to know
this, too. The Bible promises that if you seek God with all your
heart, you will find him.'

Everyone listened. Next day, every newspaper in Scotland
reported that Eric had spoken publicly about being a Christian.
From then on he gave talks in many different places, and
thousands came to hear him.

It was easy to see that Eric was different from other athletes.
At the beginning of each race, he would shake hands with all
the other runners, saying with a smile, 'Have a good race. All
the best!' Once he gave up his place on the inside, the best
position, to let a newcomer have a better chance of winning.

7

With the Olympic games less than a year away, Eric looked set to compete. He won a 100-yard race in 9.7 seconds, setting a new British record - not broken for another thirty-five years!

His most spectacular race was the 440 yards (quarter of a mile) in Stoke-on-Trent. A runner accidentally knocked Eric off the track on the first bend, leaving him behind. With a twenty-yard gap to make up, Eric leapt to his feet and thundered down the track.

With each stride he started to catch up. By the final straight he was in third place. With an almighty spurt, he shot ahead to win by two yards! The crowd were nearly hysterical with excitement. Eric collapsed, totally exhausted.

When someone later asked him the secret of his success, he replied, 'The first half I run as fast as I can, and the second I run faster with God's help.'

'I'm not running'

Eric was certain of a place in the Olympics. He was entered for both the 100 metres and the 200 metres. He trained as often as he could, while still studying for his degree, and speaking about God at meetings all over Scotland and England.

A few months before the Olympics began the timetable of events appeared. Eric was astonished! The heats for the 100 metres were on a Sunday, the Lord's day.

'I'm not running on a Sunday,' he said firmly. Eric meant it. Sunday was a day of rest.

Many people were dismayed. Eric seemed to be throwing away the chance of a gold medal for Scotland and Great Britain. Some people were very angry and called him a traitor, which hurt Eric. But he was determined: God came first.

With Eric out of the 100 metres, British hopes now rested on Harold Abrahams, a student from Cambridge University.

'This is the race for me'

Eric was now asked to train for the 400 metres instead. Much to his surprise, he found that he preferred this distance. *This is the race for me,* he thought. *If I hadn't refused to run on Sundays, I'd never have known.* But he had to beat 48 seconds to stand a chance against the other competitors. His best time was 49.6 seconds, so he pushed himself to the limit.

Saturday 5th July 1924: the eighth Olympic Games of modern times opened in Paris. These games have been held once every four years since 1896. On the Sunday when Eric could have been running in the 100 metres, he preached at a Scottish church in another part of Paris.

Next day he watched his team-mate Harold Abrahams win the semi-final and final of the 100 metres, the race Eric had been favourite to win. Harold was the first Briton ever to win this event, and Eric was delighted for him.

On Wednesday 9th July Eric lined up with Harold Abrahams and four Americans for the final of the 200 metres. Eric came third, winning a bronze medal for Great Britain, and making

history as the first Scot to win an Olympic medal for the 200
metres.

As Eric had given up the chance of winning the 100 metres,
no-one was expecting him even to qualify for the 400-metre
finals. But he did!

Going for gold
Friday 11th July – the day of the 400 metres finals. Tom, one of
the British trainers, sent Eric a note. It read: 'In the old book it
says, "He that honours me I will honour." Wishing you the best
of success always.'

Eric knew the words came from the Old Testament book of
Samuel. It reminded him of some other helpful words from the
Bible: 'Whoever believes in me will never be ashamed.'

There were six finalists, including Horatio Fitch, the
favourite and the world record holder. Eric shook hands warmly
with each man, as he always did before the race began.

The starter's pistol cracked. Eric, positioned in the outside
lane, shot straight into the lead. He was running flat out. The
Swiss runner tripped and fell. Fitch was right behind him.
Surely Eric couldn't keep up this pace?

Eric raced even faster. Head back, arms whirling he
lengthened the gap. A gasp of astonishment went up from the
crowd when, at the half-way stage, Eric was a full metre
ahead. The crowd craned forward, everyone holding their
breath, as Fitch dropped back even further. Eric broke

through the finishing tape five metres ahead! He had won the
Olympic title in a world record time of 47.6 seconds! The
crowd went wild with excitement!

The bands played, and people cheered, waved flags, clapped
and sang as Eric accepted his gold medal. As he walked back
to his dressing room, the crowd just wouldn't stop applauding.
Eric slipped quietly away to his hotel room. He had been
invited to preach at a church that weekend, and he needed
time to prepare.

Six days later Eric was back in Scotland to receive another award, his university degree. Unknown to Eric, the university also wanted to celebrate his Olympic win. When it was his turn to go up on the platform, the audience burst into applause.

Speeches were made, then some of Eric's friends lifted him on to their shoulders, carrying him out into the street, where crowds had gathered to see their hero. For weeks afterwards there were special parties, lunches and teas, with more speeches and applause.

Off to China

At one of these parties Eric made an announcement that surprised everybody. 'It's been my lifelong ambition to work in China, like my father. I've been offered a job at an Anglo-Chinese college in China, and I've accepted. I want to spend the rest of my life as a missionary.'

The following twelve months were hectic. As well as studying at Bible college in Edinburgh, Eric spent each weekend travelling all over Scotland to talk about his faith. Hundreds turned out to listen to their Olympic champion, and many decided to put God first in their lives too. Although Eric now had less time for running, he still trained and competed, breaking a few more Scottish records before he set off for China.

When the time came for Eric to leave, the huge crowds that turned out to give him a great send-off brought the traffic to a standstill in Edinburgh city centre. Eric was looking forward to seeing his family again, but he was sorry to be leaving behind all his friends.

Eric returned to China at the age of twenty-three, having left when he was just five years old. Life would be very different from now on. Summers would be hot and dry, winters icy-cold. Eric was going to live and work in Tientsin, a large industrial port in the north-east of China where his parents worked too.

14

It took Eric two weeks to reach China, travelling by train across Europe and the Soviet Union. Arriving safely, he joined his family on a seaside holiday. Proudly they listened for hours as Eric told them all that had happened since they last met.

At first Eric thought little had changed since he was a boy. The Chinese people still dressed in padded coats and many older men still wore their hair in long pigtails. But he soon discovered that the British were not very popular any more.

Many people had become angry that foreigners had so much power in China. Protest marches were organised. When British police shot and killed a peaceful demonstrator, the bad feeling increased.

At the Anglo-Chinese college, the students threatened not to return to lessons after the summer break. In Eric's first week, only a quarter of the students turned up for lessons, and several weeks passed before they all returned.

Eric found the students enjoyed his religious education lessons and his science classes. Some of them wanted to become Christians. But they were not so keen on his sports lessons.

The right clothes

The problem was that the Chinese students insisted on wearing their long blue cotton gowns for playing football and athletics, so whenever they tried to run, they tripped up. When Eric first appeared in his navy knee-length shorts and white running vest, they were shocked. Then they saw that he could move much more easily. Once they began wearing shorts, some of the students started to break athletics records.

As there was no stadium in Tientsin, Eric organised the building of a sports ground. He agreed to run at the first meeting. No-one there had seen a man run so fast before. His times were still record-breaking.

Back in Britain nobody knew that Eric was still competing, so he wasn't invited to run in the 1928 Olympics. In the week when the French and Japanese won the 200- and 400-metre races, Eric's times in China were actually faster!

The Flying Scotsman

One race that the British did hear about earned him a special nickname. Eric had been invited to run in Darien, across the bay from Tientsin. His final race was just half an hour before the last ferry sailed back. He booked a taxi to rush him to the docks as soon as the race finished.

Eric won the race and wanted to head straight for the taxi. But he had forgotten about the prize-giving, and the band was playing 'God Save the King'. (George V was on the throne then.) By the time they had finished playing, Eric only had fifteen minutes to catch his ferry!

He threw himself into the taxi and it sped away. Eric's heart sank when he arrived to see the ferry moving off. But then a gust of wind pushed the boat back towards the quay. Eric threw his bags on to the deck. *Remember how a gazelle jumps*, he told himself as he sprinted towards the gap and leapt across. Landing at the feet of some amazed passengers, he must have cleared fifteen feet between the quay and the boat! From then on Eric was known as 'The Flying Scotsman'.

Comings and goings

Time passed, and Eric's parents returned to Britain for a well-earned rest. He missed them badly. However a Canadian missionary family with two grown-up daughters, Flo (short for Florence) and Margaret, invited him to visit. Eric soon became a regular guest.

People began to notice that Eric was fond of Flo, but no-one guessed that she admired Eric too. They were both full of life and fun to be with. Flo, who was eighteen, ten years younger than Eric, planned to go to Canada to train as a nurse. Then she failed her French exam.

'Now I don't know what to do. I won't be allowed into the hospital. Maybe I should give up the idea,' she told Eric.

'You mustn't think of giving up,' he replied. 'In fact there's something else I want you to think about. Will you marry me?' Flo had no doubts. She accepted right away.

They became engaged, but it was another four years before they married, because Flo was invited to train at the hospital after all.

Meanwhile Eric returned to Scotland to train as a minister. The Scottish people hadn't forgotten him, and he was asked to speak at sports meetings, churches and colleges about his work in China. Eric studied too, and by the end of a busy year he could be called the Reverend Liddell, just like his father.

Eric spent his last few days in Scotland with his parents, as his father wasn't well enough to return to China again. It was difficult to say good-bye, not knowing when they would see each other again. On his way back to China, he visited Flo in Canada.

Eric now had new work and more travelling to do. He took church services, ran the Sunday school, acted as chairman of the games committee and took charge of the religious activities at the college.

Soon after his return, Eric had a strange experience. He was preaching in church when, for a moment, he felt that his father was standing beside him. The very next day a telegram arrived to say his father had died.

Although deeply saddened by his father's death, Eric was filled with peace, because he knew his father, who believed in Jesus, was in heaven. He also knew that his father would want him to continue his work.

Soon after, Eric heard that Flo had passed her nursing exams and was on her way back to China. Three weeks later they were married. Cards, presents and telegrams arrived from all over the world. After a holiday, they settled into their own home.

Having been separated for so long, Eric and Flo were delighted to be together. Two daughters were born, called Patricia and Heather. Eric loved being a father. But then they had a shock. Eric was asked if he would be willing to leave the college to teach in a remote Chinese village. There were no other young men available, so Eric agreed. Although he could live with his brother Robbie, who was working there as a doctor in a mission hospital, it meant leaving behind Flo and the children.

Siao Chang

The village, Siao Chang, was the very place where Eric had grown up as a child. But it was no longer a peaceful, happy village. People were hungry and frightened. Fields had been ruined by drought and locusts. Japanese soldiers had invaded the area. Chinese soldiers were fighting back, but they were also fighting each other. There were bandits, too, and stories of torture.

Eric prayed. He knew it would be dangerous, but he believed it was right to go, even though he would miss his family and life at Tientsin.

The villagers of Siao Chang gave Eric a warm welcome, especially the older people who remembered his parents. He began visiting churches and helping Chinese pastors, preaching and caring, travelling on foot or by bicycle. No matter how difficult the weather, Eric always struggled through, whether it was mud and floods, scorching heat or freezing cold.

There was the constant threat that bandits or soldiers might

attack. Eric often came across burnt-out villages, men killed and women beaten. Soldiers sometimes stopped him and bullied him, but he always stayed calm and cheerful, trying to love everyone, as Jesus taught.

Sometimes he managed to smuggle money into the hospital, by hiding it in a hollowed-out bread-roll. If the Japanese soldiers became suspicious, Eric brought out photographs of his children, which helped them forget to search him.

Once Eric found a man almost dead from a deep gash round his neck, where a Japanese soldier had tried to behead him with a sword. With Japanese planes flying overhead and with enemy troops less than a mile away, Eric and a Chinese Christian carried the man by cart to the mission hospital. The man, who recovered and later became a Christian, was an artist, and he painted many pictures for Eric because he was so grateful.

Torpedoed!

Desperate for a rest, Eric managed to take Flo and the children to Canada and Scotland for a long holiday. It was 1939, and Britain was now at war with Germany. The Liddell family had begun the long sail back to China when, just off the Irish coast, their ship was hit by a German torpedo! As damage to the ship was not serious, the captain ordered full-steam ahead. Submarines, which in those days were not so advanced as they are now, could not reach them far out at sea. They were safe.

On their return to China, Eric found people in Siao Chang were suffering even more. A high wall had been built round the village. Close to the hospital Japanese and Chinese soldiers were firing at each other. Many more people died.

As Flo was expecting another baby, and the Japanese were threatening to send all missionaries to prison camps, Eric told his wife, 'I don't want you to end up living in a camp. It would be much better if you took the children to Canada.'

'I don't want to leave,' said Flo. 'But I know it's best.' Eric

knew that even death could not separate them, and comforted Flo, saying, 'Those who love God never meet for the last time.'

Eric alone

Eric wasn't allowed back to Siao Chang, so he returned to Tientsin. For the first time in his life he had no special work to do; but he kept himself busy writing a Bible study book, beginning each morning with an hour of prayer.

A few months passed. A telegram arrived to say that he had another daughter, Maureen. Then came the news of the Japanese bombing raid on Pearl Harbor, in which many Americans died. Britain and America were now both at war with Japan.

When Japanese soldiers began ordering all missionaries to leave their homes, Eric went to live with another family. He spent his days teaching the teenage children to play tennis. From time to time letters came from Flo, and Eric couldn't help wondering, *Will I ever see my own family again?*

On 12th March 1943 Eric was told to report to a prison camp near Peking, along with all British and American people living there. Hundreds were packed into a dirty train and taken to the camp.

Prisoner

The grey camp walls were high and electrified. By night powerful searchlights beamed down from watch-towers. Japanese soldiers armed with sharp bayonets patrolled the grounds.

About 1,500 men, women and children were crammed together in this camp, including five hundred children taken from boarding schools for children whose parents were missionaries or Christian business people.

Everywhere there were queues – for the toilets, for meals, for roll-call, for chores. Frustrated and miserable, it was easy for people to quarrel. Eric spent many hours helping people to make up.

The food was very poor, mainly root vegetables and bread, and there was plenty of work to do – cleaning, cooking, mending and building. Some people who had always had servants now had to scrub floors and make fires.

As well as teaching children science and maths in the camp school, Eric also taught adults, led services in the small chapel, visited the sick, chopped wood, carried coal and water, and fetched food.

Plenty to do
Energetic but bored, the children began getting into trouble, so Eric organised plenty of sports, teaching them hockey, basketball, football, rounders and chess.

In spite of the rats, flies, dirt, disease and overcrowding, Eric was full of energy and fun. Even his brightly coloured shirts made people laugh. 'They're made from Flo's living-room curtains,' he explained, grinning broadly.

By the flickering light of a peanut-oil lamp, Eric and a room-mate studied the Bible and prayed together for an hour every morning. Eric still refused to play sport on Sundays, but when a Sunday hockey match ended in a punch-up between the children, Eric went out and acted as referee.

As the weeks became months Eric grew wearier and thinner, and he became more serious too. He began to suffer from severe headaches and could only walk with difficulty. Although he was only forty-three years old, he moved as slowly as someone twice his age.

One day he told a friend, 'I've got a splitting headache'. His friend persuaded him to see a camp doctor and to stay in the camp hospital.

'You're doing too much. Take it easy!' the doctor advised. Eric rested for a month and seemed to get better.

But the headaches wouldn't go away, and Eric found it hard to be outside in the sun. The doctors were worried. 'If only we had some equipment,' they complained. 'Then we could do some tests.'

Hope in a dark place
Eric began to feel quite sad. One evening, in the camp hospital, he began to choke and cough violently. Within minutes he was dead. Unknown to the doctors, Eric had been suffering from a brain tumour.

He was buried in an unmarked grave in the little cemetery in the camp. Every single person in the camp, including all the children, went to his funeral service. By his words and actions Eric had reminded them all of the love and kindness of Jesus, and brought hope to a dark place.

It wasn't until nearly three months later that Flo heard about Eric's death. She was deeply shocked. 'I had no idea that he was even ill!' she exclaimed.

When the news of Eric's death was announced in Scotland, people were stunned. Thousands mourned the 'Flying Scotsman' at church services all over the country. His memory lives on today as the man who refused to run on Sundays, and who brought glory to the God he loved.